Dance Grooves for Gotikara

Poems by Benjamin Kuzemka

Kansas City Spartan Press Missouri

Spartan Press
Kansas City, Missouri
spartanpresskc.com

Copyright (c) Benjamin Kuzemka, 2018
First Edition 1 3 5 7 9 10 8 6 4 2
ISBN: 978-1-946642-59-2
LCCN: 2018949522

Design, edits and layout: Jason Ryberg
Cover image: Lucy and Benjamin Kuzemka
Author photo: Lucy Kuzemka
All rights reserved. No part of this publication may be reproduced or transmitted in any form or by any means, electronic or mechanical, including photocopying, recording or by info retrieval system, without prior written permission from the author.

Spartan Press would like to thank Prospero's Books, The Fellowship of N-finite Jest, The Prospero Institute of Disquieted P/o/e/t/i/c/s, Will Leathem, Tom Wayne, Jeanette Powers, j. d. tulloch, Jon Bidwell, Jason Preu, Mark McClane, Tony Hayden and the whole Osage Arts Community.

I offer a sincere set of thank yous to the editors and supporters of Spartan Press for their support of this project, as well as those of other poets. A special thank you is owed to Jason for his tremendous care of this collection.

These pieces never would have made it off their post-it notes without Ray's counsel and friendship, in addition to the support of Matthew, Erin, Tim, Jorden, Mary, and the people at *U City Review*. Thank you.

To my family, thank you for your hope and constant charity.

To my wife, thank you for teaching me how to dance.

— BK

CONTENTS

I eat Sun Chips when I pray / 1

I only trust a god who remembers / 2

These days I read the Four Quartets backward / 3

In love, she was something / 4

She was a real rubster / 5

I still spend odd hours / 6

A weeknight bleeds across the Beltway / 7

Early evening hands find boat sides / 8

This heaven is heaven / 9

A sister tugs open the chapel blinds / 11

A summer shower / 12

I sit with the rabbits and the rocks / 13

This late morning sinks in / 14

Life / 15

There's a barren moor out there hiding / 16

Yes, yes— / 17

I'm so very tired / 18

Nothing surprising happens in Blackbird / 19

Its Saturday night and I'm itching for some soteria / 21

The morning turns inward / 22

I sit on my knees / 23

We sit. Watching blondes run through rain / 24

I glared at an oriole on a power line / 25

A half moon / 27

A tin boat rocks / 28

Earlier I was a handful of hours / 29
I don't believe in fate / 30
You can be the hairdresser / 31
This is Pentecost / 32
A couple compares shallots / 33
America is my dharma / 34
I spend most days avoiding / 36
Another night churning / 37
Middle of the winter / 38
I walk through the closing streets / 39
The power which pulls us to a stranger's wake / 41
Implicit with the idea of original sin / 44
They say that you can hear nothing / 45
With you, I saw the world never end / 47
I once said good morning to a ghost / 48
I once fell asleep in a cave / 49
I once spun Bix / 50
I once forgot that I lied / 51
I once sung Cole Porter in the shower / 52
No amount of this now-warm belgian / 53
I sit lazily in the back of the chapel / 54
A seminarian once told me / 55
This house was built for me / 56
Saint Joseph, pray for me / 57
God became god / 60

According to the Pali canon, Gotikara was a friend and confidant of Kassapa Buddha, the ancient predecessor of Gautama, the Buddha of our current age. He lived humbly, supporting his family with his work as a potter. In the modern Theravada tradition, he is sometimes revered as saint and a model grihastin, or householder, who lived in a constant awareness of dharma and its relationship with one's own capacity for lasting sukha, or happiness.

-BK

I

1.

I eat Sun Chips when I pray;
I stare at peeling birches,
the blank screens, the air
conditioning units.

Oh, and yes God answers.
She's no prude when it comes to suggestions.

Juan Cruz was just listening too hard.
Saints are all like that— expecting
God to be a god
and not a tad bored,
vaguely hangry.

2.

I only trust a god who remembers
that I need more than mere salvation,

which like all things
is magnified
by a story, a good clove of garlic,
a magnificent slap on the ass.

My epochs are the most real
and impermanent of things.

I can convince neither
you nor me
of our utter unabstraction.

But do let November come.

3.

These days I read the *Four
Quartets* backward.

I know so well how
a wash machine settles into place.

Most of this world's grandparents
are dead; we play with their bonds
and their ottomans
and gladly never dream.

—

I look at our pumpkins
and the photos of us picking
the pumpkins

and a chubby little squirrel
beckons my wrist,
whispers *again.*

4.

In love, she was something
of an Argentinian Nazi—

upset, unconfused,
no longer a slave to stomach ailments.

She's the reason
I sometimes drink decaf.

She's my chin-up mentor,
my Aunt Lorelai.

—

Sometimes I wonder
if the saints regret as little as I do.

And they only appear to
humans when needed.

That's why I
never heard Gotikara

before
I saw her.

5.

She was a real rubster
of the Olive Garden variety—
the stuff plain Hershey bars
are made of.

I imagine her still happy
and hating my back hair.

I study all the fruit futures,
the pierced bellies.

Am I still a gracious host?
Have I forgotten the feel
of a coffee grinder come midnight?

6.

I still spend odd hours
explaining to the angels my human needs.

God, they know,
is at their mercy, too.

Coffee creamer falls, fades away.
Together, we play Keith Jarrett
and wrapping-paper jams.

I've given all the angels names

and I pretend to remember them
and the cheddar pretends to suffice.

I am immortal, I swear.
Can they not read my tattoo?
Can you?

7.

A weeknight bleeds across the Beltway.

French gin, drying foreheads,
a half moon and a baseball game.
A belated decade.

It's as if the sorbet's
been dry-cleaned out of the sherry.

All that's left is
some supercritical gunk
and discounted fish oil tablets.

—

I cherish my photos of the church
where the kind folks still humped to
Come Sail Away,
fingering ornery
pistachios and choking back
almost alien tears.

Tip your server, yes. But know that
every distant god is near.

8.

Early evening hands find boat sides,
cotton pockets, truffled dips.

This marina shack has long ago
priced me into a flourish.

No one here could guess at how
unlonely I am.

I can hear my wife so many
glossy miles inland.

Tonight, I can let this world make
its bellies glad.

My love's arms are simply that strong;
she has the strongest of arms.

9.

This heaven is heaven.
This one.

These hands have known and kneaded God.
He twice dissolved on these tongues.
He twice got my Starbucks order right.

Gotikara knew well to limit paradise
to the wiring in a knock-off Stratocaster.

God, that gluten tug,
is the child who enters the kiln.

II

10.

A sister tugs open the chapel blinds,
her sister naps in a wheelchair.

Damp from the rain
I watch the mountains or the altar
or the ground.

11.

A summer shower
falls upon the thin roof
of the abbey's library.

I set my book
down a daydream ago
to watch the foothills
soften.

Afternooned eyes
latch onto bookbindings.

Maybe I'll microwave the coffee.

I've never grasped a scenery.

12.

I sit with the rabbits and the rocks
sifting through
the dreams which granulate my days—

dreams which bind me
to futures I've long since disavowed
and which distort all of my suggestive pasts.

With me sit no ghosts
no angry ancestors.
My dreams destroyed them some summer ago.

I sit with the rocks and the bunny rabbits.

13.

This late morning sinks in
relapsing, dressing
after an hour or two of clutching
Ikea furniture for dear sustenance.

Footsteps explore the second bedroom;
I hunch into the sofa
quite ignorant of all musics
and too passive to light the stove.

A passing Hyundai, a punch of gust—
no, these rooms will never dry.

14.

Life
it seems to me

is
in desperate

need of a proper
subtitle.

15.

There's a barren moor out there hiding
humping teenagers as they listen to Radiohead and
sip local vodka and stolen trippel.

Someday they will weep with the blood
and the biscuits for that impotent decade.

This, of course, is why men wear mustaches.

16.

Yes, yes—
we sipped coffee at midnite because we half thought
Jesus might appear
like he used to.

Why couldn't he pop into a suburban Thursday?

That's one god who could wear the shit out of white after Labor Day.

17.

I'm so very tired.

Gods have legions
and saints have confidence.

All we get are half
marathon bumper stickers

and eternity,
that participation prize.

So *Ad te venio,*
but only because I have to.

18.

Nothing surprising happens in *Blackbird*,
save the pause at the end.

I used to play *Blackbird* well.

I used to love
all the things
I still love.

Anyhow, it's too late.
I found God some other way.

III

19.

ジャズ

Its Saturday night and I'm itching for some soteria.
But Jazu only makes sense on a weekday
when it bounces forth
both wrong and raw.

Untimeliness is essential.

Tonight even Coltrane's a bumpkin,
Evans slashes about in the scratchy background
waiting for a solo that will never arrive.

Tonight I'm like everyone else—
just trying to find something funky
to toss into my Sprite cans.

20.

The morning turns inward
checking her breasts for lumps.

A rosary has been nailed to
the bare drywall.
The beads were weaved by some
Vietnamese Norbertines
but have never been touched
with human hands.

Outside in the heat a
washing machine rumbles away
trying fruitlessly to shake off last night's funk.

21.

I sit on my knees
translating my own poems into Urdu.

My green ink can't keep up
with the sheer sobriety of the timid rhymes.

—

The smoothness of numbers
never fails to turn me on,
yet its ink, like science,
never givers more than an accidental
tease.

22.

We sit. Watching blondes run through rain,
their laughter sculpting something real
from a vague boulevard.

I love business districts past midnight.
Fried dumplings, beer. A man too drunk to think.
No sunlight for miles.

Us, almost alone,
waiting for froth to vanish.

We don't speak; we haven't for days.
We've driven through Latvia, stalinesque and restless.

Something has halted us here.

Our forearms bend, pretend
to follow the teenage footsteps
which always find a puddle.
The man stands up, but stays with the sauerkraut
under the marquee.

Our father loved *Fun, Fun, Fun,*
but now we both might know
that he just wanted a Firebird.

23.

I glared at an oriole on a power
line for seven minutes today.

He flew off into the neighboring plot.

He will die before me
and has no fucking idea.

IV

24.

A half moon
in late afternoon—

the ear of a god who misses me
who misses you.

25.

A tin boat rocks
against the confines of Lake Victoria
and my ears chew kachumbari
and wait for the punchline.

26.

Earlier I was a handful of hours
into a hello sunday morning.

I drove windows-down through the former war zone
and heard only
the absence of wind
and competing church bells.

27.

I don't believe in fate,
but I still accept most invitations.

I've golfed on six continents,
and birdied on five.

—

The store owner smiles, somewhat
embarrassed.
He is my contact with today.

I return to the North Chinese streets,
confident with potato chips and pickled beets.

Nietzsche, Emerson, saw eternal truths
as human projections,
but I swear that when

I met God,
she was a potter, too.

28.

You can be the hairdresser
and I can be your vision.

When together we contemplate
the tao,
who will sigh?
or pour another?

29.

This is pentecost.
This rain can't keep

pace with the morning.
I am that statue of Mary.

I've grown rogue and soft.
This is the sequence. This

is the endless song.
Is spirit real? I can't

read my answer, for it is
relentlessly pentecost.

And we are hurtling into each other,
you and I. The dance

won't stop until we're
spent and wet.

30.

A couple compares
shallots, pokes at fruit,
don't hold my gaze.

An April evening has careened
into the market. I pour
wine, work on stats homework,

think hockey thoughts. I'm
protected by my sweatshirt,
stretched thin with sabi.

I can continue. The cashier
is the owner's daughter,
offers discounted seeds.

The world is waiting for all of us
here. Like Vermeer it waits,
knows.

31.

America is my dharma. And it is
better than yours.

I can be so rich,
so rich I can scream.

I have favorite pincer maneuvers,
favorite philosophies and behavioral therapies.

I have fugues and tacos,
Wilco albums and ports of call in Spain.

I make the best travel plans,
because I've had so much practice.

My molecules coagulated here, in this
Midwest, away from Austerlitz,

with no extraneous chromosomes or cares.
I'm so rich I can afford poetry.

My life is the first and third acts of a rom-com,
and I love American loves.

They're all that I bothered to keep.
It's the sheer weight of a make-believe world

forged by my great-aunts and uncles
exhausted by disbelief.

I am forged in a crockpot,
an utter angel,

angry,
with well-rubbed eyes.

32.

I spend most days avoiding
software updates. I read

about Stalingrad
or eat barbecue sauce.

In my selfies, I have the look of a man
looking for the nearest bathroom.

I'm always early. I found out
everything about God

and God is a pivot table.
I live well and I have the proof.

I have the smudges left by this vestibular place.
I will always order extra breadsticks.

I remember March, I remember when
belly became my favorite color.

33.

Another night churning
testing bedsheets and
minor chords

and crumpled philosophies,
latching into splendid ideas

sprinting away from others.
More trucks slide by on the biway.

More future gods and saints
busied like me with cheeseburgers

and tomorrows.

I think about tomorrow,
but I can't begin to believe in it.

It will come despite my agnosticism
and again shake me with surprise

and will again pass into another
and again I'll consent,

but I cannot consent yet.

34.

Middle of the winter, my
window open. This is how I once
eloped with contingency.

My back snug to the wall,
resting on bluegrass.
The cul-de-sac

has six inches
of snow, with a seventh
coming down slow,

drawn by the streetlamp.
I used to write parcels,
Chinese and honest,

scribblings to the moon
and the things she loves.
My ghost is here.

It's all some wake from unsorted
evenings when I knew
the present so well.

35.

I walk through the closing
streets painted

red with guitars
and street vendors.

I try to hold on to Beijing.
I rub her salt into my palms.

Cars pass by, thankful and quick
and boys tell girls jokes.

I want to be the spider
who haunts this place.

V

36.

The power which pulls us to a stranger's wake
is a strange and moonlit power.

I suspect that most of the handshakes were those
of strangers—
the protesters outside, the supporters, the
Freemasons, the Knights of
Columbus, kind folks from the union,
a politician or three, the pastor. As for me,

I was driving around
avoiding my two-bedroom flat when I came across
the hundreds of cars parked on Gravois.
The floodlights, the police lights. The protesters,
and so on.

A political wake, I suppose. Intentional or not. Made
possible because some well methed bumpkin
pulled a gun on this man who I will never know, nor
would have known,
and squeezed.

I shook no one's hand.
My thoughts were far from profound—
mostly concerned with
the cheerleader widow who nodded

silent salutations. I avoided the tiny
eyes of the toddler, who was vaguely aware that there's
two permanent holes in daddy's tummy tonight.

—

A month has passed.
I pass tattered blue ribbons throughout the south city
and his portrait is advertised at the gun outlet
on my drive to work.

—

But this tonight
a cozy hundred hours later my thoughts turn to
that dead man
and sometimes even poets have something to say.
Nothing personal, of course.
Nothing real nor anything of solace or substance.
Just me feeling how the events that aren't mine have
digested in my flimsy, remotive hands.

And I don't love cops —
too many innocent crimes for that —
but those same crimes
have shown me most of purgatory.
And so I dream secure dreams.
And yes,
if your life goal is to not be shot,
then become an accountant.

But regardless of words and sermons and accolades,
now this stranger is floating around in a place very
different than Shaw Avenue with only the

frozen custard fundraisers, stranger rosaries,
and pride and dwindling memories,
to hold up the toddler and mommy.

And,
sitting here in this airport bar waiting
for Lovely to get off work, I'm aware that

me — white,
rich, brilliant, almost handsome — am
the reason that Officer Schlemmer had to die.

37.

Implicit with the idea of original sin
is the idea
that sin
and destiny
are the same goblin.

38.

They say that you can hear nothing in
the black vastness of space.

But I suspect God hears his step-children.

He hears them as they whimper
and roar.

I [continued]

39.

With you, I saw the world never end.

I saw millstones for Oltec dreams,
and coffee mugs with our faces on them.

My roommate won't stop tuning her acoustic
electric. She gave me this

message that's lighter than bird bones—
a Nephite monstrosity made of salmon and stock yields.

She gave me a Borders gift card
There are no words, no rings in the wood.

I still remember the cricket matches in Pune,
the quick alley Kingfishers, the Starbucks in the lobby,

the apocalyptic worries, Sanskrit lessons,
and pull out methods.

I bartered and bartered for that handknit shawl,
and still I didn't pay enough.

In another lifetime
I could've been Jesus' favorite headrest.

Instead, I got kicked out of a cult.

40.

I once said good morning to a ghost
who hollered back at me

some some jazz
standard I'd heard long ago.

No one wants to be an animal—
we're just welded that way,

relentlessly together.

41.

I once fell asleep in a cave,
shivering.

Only had that torn up copy of à Kempis to keep
me safe from the decaying July.

42.

I once spun Bix
Beiderbecke on the turntable
and redacted all past promises
with a glob of blue ink
and understood
instantly who willed the other Kennedy.

43.

I once forgot that I lied and ended up getting my caesar salad kicked in the back of a Greek diner.

44.

I once sung Cole Porter in the shower.
Then I became holy,
then I became saturnine,

then I met her
and now I sing Cole Porter again.

45.

No amount of this now-warm belgian
can erase the fact that God
once told Zephaniah that war rape was cool.

That means that he watched the Eastern front and
Nanking with a bowl of buttered celestial popcorn
not even watching the commercials flashing between
our precious little wars
and hemorrhaging genitalia.

One of those singing reality shows was on BBC4
and its well known that he never misses an episode.

46.

I sit lazily in the back of the chapel
chewing
thoughtfully
on my father's cancer.

It's a nice chapel.
Slovenian tourists come and take
photographs of the famed mosaic
and the icon of Mary, Queen
of Peace.

A thought comes and bores me. The priest
will soon walk in,
pronounce the Angelus,
and begin the dance party
that rages in the gentle
guise of a deposition.

47.

A seminarian once told
me to love Christ,

to love him like a brother.

Maybe the kid was right, but
in a multiple choice sort of way.

It's quite possible to love Christ,
and not trust him.

48.

This house was built for me.
1893 was a good year, a great vintage.
Sharecroppers and magicians dreamt
of these fine bricks.
They slaved for these bookcases and spice racks.
They had paprika dreams and ate unvirtual mush.

If I could return my birthright to a worthy
world I would.
But I'd ask for the Raj in return.
I'd be a filibuster for Beatle bootlegs,
and share everything, save my style.

I think I'm just tired.
All I can afford is last year's grapes,
and they taste like softballs and shit.

Love has been quite the sonata to something
strange
and forthcoming.

I suspect that I'll accidently die for that one furry thing—
an annuity holder capable of baptizing
every ghost.

49.

Saint Joseph, pray for me,
that I soon somehow know
which heavens are real.

Like you, I've heard the voice of God.
I've had your ladder dreams and know what it is
to pray to a vase.

Saint Joseph, you offer reproach, not
friendship. Parliaments
in lieu of life lessons.

Thank you for your shoulders and arms
and how with them
you keep us all at a holy arm's length.

When I'm with your son, I
hear your disbelief.
He can do better than me and usually does.

He could've been that quarterback
without my clan,
and spoke Spanish like you.

Pray for me, as you've always done.
Pray with the gestures
you alone remember.

I need everything this life has been trying
to give me. I've
torn my only net.

If you've the time, remember them
all. It is Tuesday in the lowlands;
it is Tuesday again.

—

I remember you from my
youth—
angry, like ice.

I am no one's father, so there.
We built a shelf,
bought a vice, a drillbit,
and our favorite Szechuan takeout.

Saint Joseph, when you pray
for us speak louder. Oh,
and can I be like you?

Saint Joseph, I love you.
I sit now on your side of the aisles,
and eat your brand of potato chips.

I need something more, and
so you still wheeze. Pray,
pray and control my climate.

I've never missed you and never will
have to. This is the ache,
the calligraphy.

Please hold my dad's hand.
Make it less ashy.

This distance is church.
You've shattered my ankles.
I am here.

50.

God became god

when he became
the only god

to wish upon herself
a never ending lifetime

of unrequited love.

Benjamin Kuzemka is from suburban Chicago. He spent the first part of his twenties on a handful of continents and then joined a religious order. He left seminary, met a girl, and now lives in Saint Louis, Missouri.

This project was made possible, in part, by generous support from the Osage Arts Community.

Osage Arts Community provides temporary time, space and support for the creation of new artistic works in a retreat format, serving creative people of all kinds — visual artists, composers, poets, fiction and nonfiction writers. Located on a 152-acre farm in an isolated rural mountainside setting in Central Missouri and bordered by ¾ of a mile of the Gasconade River, OAC provides residencies to those working alone, as well as welcoming collaborative teams, offering living space and workspace in a country environment to emerging and mid-career artists. For more information, visit us at www.osageac.org

www.ingramcontent.com/pod-product-compliance
Lightning Source LLC
Chambersburg PA
CBHW021450080526
44588CB00009B/781